D0324268

Life Could Be Verse

Life Could Be Verse

reflections on love, loss,
and what really matters

Kirk Douglas

Health Communications, Inc.
Deerfield Beach, Florida

www.hcibooks.com

**Library of Congress Cataloging-in-Publication Data
is available through the Library of Congress**

© 2014 The Bryna Company

ISBN-13: 9780757318474 (Paperback)
ISBN-10: 0757318479 (Paperback)
ISBN-13: 9780757318481 (ePub)
ISBN-10: 0757318487 (ePub)

Publisher: Health Communications, Inc.
            3201 S.W. 15th Street
            Deerfield Beach, FL 33442-8190

Cover design by Larissa Hise Henoch
Interior design and formatting by Larissa Hise Henoch and Lawna Patterson Oldfield

For the woman I have been
married to for 60 years.
Anne, I love you.

FOREWORD

Friends,

From the first day we met, I knew right away that Kirk Douglas was a man of captivating energy and tremendous talent. I personally love Kirk in tights yelling, "I am Spartacus!"

I'm honored he thought of me for the foreword.

In his latest book, *Life Could Be Verse*, we are given a very touching and heartfelt glimpse into his life through poetry.

He has been writing poetry since he was eight years old, and from those poems we are able to gather great wisdom and feel his passion for life and family. I hope you enjoy Kirk's book of poetry—providing you know how to read!

Each poem is an original and can only be expressed by someone who's lived a very long and fruitful life. His personal experiences are those that many of us can relate to in our lives. His life is an inspiration to everyone. The times spent with his beautiful, loving, and caring wife Anne are always a delight.

Kirk is not only an American icon of the screen but a very loving man. I am honored to call him my friend.

Please buy the book. The word's out. . . . Kirk needs money!

Enjoy,

Don Rickles

ACKNOWLEDGMENTS

A SUDDEN STROKE caused me to lose my speech, but I didn't lose my mind. It made me ask questions about myself. Is that ego? I don't know.

Throughout my life I have written poems that express my true feelings. While reading them for this book, I came a little bit closer to understanding who I really am.

I don't like doing anything alone; I always seek help, and this book was no different.

Grace Eboigbe, my assistant, impressed me with her editing skill and creativity. She helped me immensely. I thank her.

David Bender is a professional journalist who became my friend. His comments were also helpful and I thank him, too.

Allison Janse, HCI editor, and her colleague Larissa Henoch surprised me by their acute comments. I thank them as well.

Actors are children,

Who refuse to grow up.

They live in a land of make-believe.

They play sailors, soldiers, and cowboys, too.

They're happy when they deceive.

Hard work can get you fame and fortune,

And maybe make you a star.

But nothing will make you happy

Until you know who you are.

Most of my life was spent as an actor who never took the time to know who he really was. For years, I lived in a land of make-believe, slipping in and out of characters for ninety films. I have flubbed just as many scenes in my "real life" as I have in the "reel life" of my films.

In 1996, I suffered a debilitating stroke that rendered me speechless. *An actor who can't talk,* I thought. *Is this the end?* This caused me to take inventory of my life and ask questions like, "Who am I?" At the age of 98, I am still looking. I know that I have made mistakes and I have my share of regrets. But overall, life has been very good to me. As they say in Yiddish, "It could be verse."

Poetry has been a part of my life from an early age. From schoolyard rhymes to love sonnets, my verses have helped me woo some leading ladies, deal with rejections on screen and off, and even to find my voice again after my stroke. Now, I am happy to share my love of poetry with my grandchildren, who also like to write. Writing is a gift that I hope will stay with them long after I am not.

Here I share some of my memories and the poems they inspired. We'll travel back in time to old Hollywood, when times were simpler. I hope you enjoy the journey. . . .

I GREW UP IN AMSTERDAM, NEW YORK, a small town northwest of Albany and Schenectady. My family lived in the last house on the road near the mill and the railroad tracks. I was the only son, in the middle of six sisters. My father emigrated from Russia and couldn't find work in the mills. So, he got himself a horse and a wagon and became a ragman, buying and reselling old rags, pieces of scrap, and junk for pennies. Even in our poor neighborhood, the ragman was the lowest rung on the ladder. And I was the ragman's son.

Pa spent most of his time in the saloon, drinking and fascinating his friends with his stories. I would often sneak in the back and watch everybody listening to Pa, mesmerized; he was such a showman.

But my mother was the one who told me my favorite story.

She was in the kitchen, stirring a pot of soup.

I asked her, "Ma, how was I born?" She wiped her hands on her apron and scooped me up on her lap.

"Well, Issur," she said (that's my real name), "it was a sunny winter morning when I saw something out of the window. I looked out and saw a beautiful gold box shimmering in the snow. It was carved with fruits and flowers and suspended from heaven by thin silver strands."

"A gold box?!"

"Yes, a gold box. I threw on my shawl, rushed into the yard, and opened it."

"What was in it? What was in it?"

"You!"

"Me?"

"Yes, you! Naked. I wrapped you in my shawl and ran back into the house."

"But, Ma, what about the box?"

"I don't know. When I looked out the window again, it was gone."

"But, Ma, why didn't you grab the box and keep it?"

"Issur, when I found you I was so happy that I couldn't think about anything else."

"You lost the gold box?!"

"Issur, when I found you I was so happy that I couldn't think about anything else."

My mother—she is worth more than any gold box.

WHEN I WAS IN SECOND GRADE, I got a part in the school play. I played the lead, the shoemaker in *The Shoemaker and the Elves.* Ma was thrilled. She made me a little black apron that tied in the back. On stage, I proudly sang the song I'd memorized:

> *I'm Tack Hammer*
> *The shoemaker*
> *I work on shoes*
> *All day*

Of course, my mother and sisters were there to watch me. But when I looked out from the stage, I was stunned. My father was standing in the back of the auditorium. He was a gruff man who usually ignored me, but not this time. After the play, he took me out and bought me a vanilla ice cream cone. I felt like my father recognized me for the first time. That cone was better than any Oscar.

In high school I was introduced to poetry. It intrigued me—until the English teacher announced, "I want all of you to write a short poem."

Holy Moses! What the hell did I even know about writing?! My parents could barely speak English, and now I was expected to put words together that rhymed. I didn't know what to do. I'd always dreamed about seeing the ocean and going out on a big sailing ship. It was a wonderful trip only in my imagination. The farthest I had ever traveled was to the big city of Schenectady, fifteen miles away.

So I decided to write about things I never knew:

The Discarded Ship

Above me have flown many flags

But now my sails are torn to rags

My bows are white from swirling foam

As o'er the many seas I roam

But now there's nothing left for me

I live in days that used to be.

AFTER GRADUATING FROM HIGH SCHOOL, I kissed my crying mother good-bye (my father was at the saloon), and I hitchhiked to St. Lawrence University in Canton, New York, with $164 in my pocket. I filled out an application, and, surprisingly, the school accepted me. My first class was Shakespeare. I loved to listen to the teacher recite the many sonnets.

But more than that, I liked to look at the girl who sat in front of me. She had flaming red hair. She always looked straight ahead and followed the professor while I stared at the back of her head. For the first time in my life, a strange feeling came over me. I fell in love. This is what I wrote to get her attention:

How Oft Have I Sat Behind Thee

How oft have I sat behind thee

In awe and watched thy titian hair

Resplendent in the rays

Of morning's golden light,

Which danced about thy head

For joy, a gorgeous sight!

Each ray thus shaped

A sparkling diadem

Of jewels to crown

You queen of beauty over all.

Bewitched by a vision so fair,

I reached out and touched your hair.

Happily you turn, smile at me—

And change my humble state to ecstasy.

Two lovers with some friends.

It worked! We had a blissful relationship for two years. We were head over heels in love, together every day. But then she dumped me.

She had fallen for another boy at the neighboring college. I was heartbroken. I still gazed at her auburn hair, but she never turned around again. I was miserable.

Rejection

Most love affairs, it's sad but true

Bring grief for one and joy for two.

One heart is broken, while two are gay,

Two hearts beat in rapture—while one pines away.

It's fair enough, you will agree

To sacrifice one heart for two.

It's fair enough, my friend—unless

The broken heart belongs to you.

I tried to blot out the image of her beautiful hair. It was not easy. At night, the magical stars I saw were in her eyes; in the white clouds I saw her face. *Am I going to see her everywhere?* I wondered. But one night, I saw a full moon, without any trace of her.

Pale Moon

Pale ghostly moon on a field of white

Moving so stealthily through the night

Silently fading beneath the black

As onward you go on your track.

Beaming so softly a fragile light

As you glide over clouds in your sight.

Tell me what you see,

On the Earth below.

What are the secrets

That you alone know?

With a grin on your face

You silently pass by

Fading away into the morning sky.

AFTER COLLEGE, I went to New York City and applied for a scholarship at the American Academy of Dramatic Arts, one of the best dramatic schools in the country. They turned me down. Not to be deterred, I applied to another drama school and they were happy to take me. After two days of study there, I received a note from AADA. They were giving me a scholarship. It was difficult to tell the headmaster of my second-choice school that I was leaving, but I hurried to the Academy. There, I studied Stanislavsky and all of the great actors.

Now, I was ready to tackle Broadway.

My first audition was for the legendary Mae West. She was a stage actor who became famous in Hollywood for the pictures *She Done Him Wrong* and *I'm No Angel.* She was known for her luscious sex appeal. Remember her line? "It's not the men in your life that matters; it's the life in your men." My agent sent me to her apartment on the fifteenth floor of the Essex House; my palms were sweating as I rang the bell.

I entered her living room; it was filled with tall, burly young men. At only five feet eleven inches, I felt like a midget. Suddenly, the room became silent as Mae West descended the stairs like a queen, her ample bosom squeezed beneath a form-fitting black negligee. Her eyes scanned the room and stopped on me. "Thank you for coming. You can go now," she said with a dismissive smile. My first rejection.

Suddenly, the room became silent as Mae West descended the stairs like a queen . . .

As time went on, I faced many more rejections, but I did land a few bit parts in plays that didn't last long. I was an understudy in *Kiss and Tell*, produced by George Abbott, the biggest producer on Broadway. One evening backstage, he asked me, "Kirk, can you sing?"

"Sing? I sang a song in college."

"What was the song?"

"It's called 'Red Hot Henry Brown.'"

He laughed, "Well, can you still sing it?"

"What do you mean?"

"I'm having auditions for my musical *On the Town*. Be there at three o'clock." He walked away.

I didn't know if I could pull it off, but I thought, *What the hell? What's the worst thing that can happen—they'll laugh at me? I can handle that.* So at three o'clock I showed

Mae West, *She Done Him Wrong*.

up backstage. The theater was empty except for a small group of people that included George Abbott, Leonard Bernstein, and the writers Betty Comden and Adolph Green. They were listening intently to another young actor singing for the same part. He was good. When he finished, a voice said, "Thank you." Then another voice called: "Kirk Douglas!" I took a deep breath and walked out onstage. A man asked, "What are you going to sing?"

George Abbott interrupted, "Red Hot Henry Brown!"

Everyone laughed, but the piano player said, "I don't know that song."

Cockily I said, "I don't need music." I began to sing it:

Take a look at me, if you want to see
A man that's steppin' about;
I go in cafes so fast, I meet myself comin' out.
Ev'ry body's heard about me, all over town,
Girls can't tame me, they nick-name me,
Hottest man around!

As I was singing, I looked out into the nearly empty theater. George Abbott was watching me with a little smile. Leonard Bernstein leaned over and said something to Comden and Green. *Was this working?*

Then, my big finish:

> *I'm Red Hot Henry Brown,*
> *The hottest man in town,*
> *That red hot mamma that you heard about,*
> *Took a look at me, and her fire went out,*
> *I'm a man that's hard to find,*
> *'Cause I'm the red hot steppin' kind*
> *They call me Red Hot Henry, Red Hot Henry . . .*

"That's enough, Kirk!" Startled, I turned and began to leave the stage, dejectedly.

"Be at the rehearsal room tomorrow morning." That stopped me. I looked at George Abbott in disbelief. "You've got the part! Be at rehearsal at 10:00 AM tomorrow."

I was ecstatic when I entered the rehearsal room. I imagined my name in lights. The song I was going to learn was a beautiful song, "Lonely Town." I started to sing.

A town's a lonely town,
When you pass through
And there is no one waiting there for you,
Then it's a lonely town.
You wander up and down,
The crowds rush by,
A million faces pass before your eye,
Still it's a lonely town.

But then came the line:

Unless there's love
A love that's shining like a harbor light

It was in a high key and I couldn't reach it. We tried again, but I couldn't hit that note. I kept on trying and trying until the pianist finally said, "That's enough for today."

The next day I woke up with laryngitis and they gave the part to someone else. My body had rejected me. Sometimes, you can't win for losing.

HITLER INTERRUPTED MY SERIES OF REJECTIONS. My short naval career began in 1943 and ended in 1944 in San Diego. I immediately made plans to go back to New York.

Meanwhile, I had heard that Lauren Bacall was making her first picture in Hollywood, *To Have and Have Not.* Lauren and I dated briefly in drama school when she was known as Betty. I found her phone number and called her. We made a date to meet at a restaurant. I was on time, still wearing my naval uniform. Betty came in with a script under her arm.

"What's that?" I asked.

"I have a wonderful part."

I thumbed through the script. "What part do you play?"

Betty took the script, turned to an earmarked page, and began to read:

> "You know you don't have to act with me, Steve. You don't have to say anything, and you don't have to do anything. Not a thing. Oh, maybe just whistle. You know how to whistle, don't you, Steve? You just put your lips together and . . . blow."

"Betty, you're going to be a star."

Back in New York, I started auditioning again (no singing) and landed the lead in *The Wind Is Ninety*. After we opened I waited anxiously to see what the critics would say. The *New York Times* wrote, "Kirk was nothing short of superb." Being an insecure actor, my reaction was, *Why* "nothing"? *Why didn't he just say Kirk Douglas was superb?!* Despite my insecurity, the play was a hit.

In Hollywood, Bacall ran into the producer Hal Wallis at a party. He was on his way to New York to cast his next picture. Wallis was a big deal—he had produced films like *Casablanca* and *The Maltese Falcon* and had made Betty's beau (and future husband), Humphrey Bogart, a star.

"Hal," Betty said, taking his arm. "I want to tell you about a friend of mine who's doing a play in New York. His name is Kirk Douglas. . . ."

Hall Wallis came to the Booth Theatre and saw my performance. Afterward, he ventured backstage and offered me a part in *The Strange Love of Martha Ivers* with Barbara Stanwyck and Van Heflin.

The Strange Love of Martha Ivers. Barbara Stanwyck and Van Heflin tried to kill me—without success.

My first publicity still with Barbara Stanwyck. Do I look scared?

On the train, on the way to California, I kept studying the lines of the script, *The Strange Love of Martha Ivers*. I was so immersed that I didn't pay attention to the vast American countryside whizzing by me. I didn't care. When I arrived in Los Angeles we were set to start rehearsing the next day.

The read-through took place in a large, empty rehearsal hall in the studio. We all sat around a table, with scripts in our hands. I made a point of closing my script and got ready to impress them. I recited my lines with feeling but was suddenly interrupted by a voice, "Hey! What the hell are you doing?" I looked up to the scowling face of the star, Van Heflin.

"What's wrong?" I asked.

I got my face dirty in *Champion*.

"Wrong?! You're saying my lines! That's what's wrong!"

In all my excitement, I had been studying the role of the lover instead of the hus-band. I apologized and picked up the script as I tried not to hear the tittering laughter of Barbara Stanwyck.

After *The Strange Love of Martha Ivers*, I filmed a few more pic-

Just before I got knocked out in *Champion*.

tures: *Out of the Past* and *A Letter to Three Wives*—but none of them had the impact of *Champion*. I played Midge, a young boxer. It was a very physical part—lots of boxing and rope-skipping. Fortunately, I had been a champion wrestler in college, so I could deal with the physical activity.

It amazes me how many things I have had to learn in my career—trick horseback riding (for *Lonely Are the Brave*, *The Indian Fighter*, and *Along the Great Divide*); juggling (for *The Juggler*); swinging on a trapeze (for *The*

The things you do for a paycheck (and an Oscar nomination).

Marilyn Maxwell and me in *Champion*.

Story of Three Loves); running across outstretched oars (for *The Vikings*); and many others.

After I filmed *Champion* I began to get some great parts, among them *Ace in the Hole,* directed by my

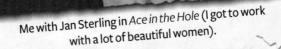

Me with Jan Sterling in *Ace in the Hole* (I got to work with a lot of beautiful women).

The "ace" in the hole.

I always read the comics.

friend Billy Wilder, and *Detective Story*. I prepared for *Detective Story* by working as a police officer in New York City, booking criminals. But my favorite memory was when I did *The Bad and the Beautiful*.

At our first rehearsal, I looked across the table at beautiful Lana Turner. *Jeez! I get PAID to make love to her!*

I enjoyed playing the scenes with Lana. Not only was she easy on the eyes, she was a much better actress than I realized. But, one of the best

Jeez! I get PAID to make love to her!

moments was our last scene together when I dumped her—fully clothed—into the swimming pool. Lana took it in stride, swimming underwater in her evening gown and coming up on the opposite side.

My friend Boit.

MY FAME WAS RISING. In 1958, they sent me to London to shoot *The Devil's Disciple* with Burt Lancaster. I have done five movies with Burt, or "Boit" as I used to call him. He called me "Koik." Before we started filming, Burt and I were intimidated about working with Laurence Olivier, an incredible actor. But we needn't have worried, he turned out to be a great guy.

While we were in London, Burt and I were asked to perform a skit at the Palladium for the Motion Picture Relief Fund charity gala. We did a song and dance routine dressed as Englishmen, singing "Maybe It's Because I'm a Londoner That I Love London So."

I learned a lot working with Larry in *The Devil's Disciple*.

"Excuse me, Eleanor, but you're ripping my shirt."

Me, playing the smart alec.

Detective Story with Eleanor Parker.

AFTER A FEW MORE MOVIES AND PLAYS, I got an offer that I couldn't refuse: A movie in France! I had never been to Paris and I was excited. With my bag packed, I was waiting in the hotel in New York for my car to take me to the airport. Even though I was happy, I felt a bit lonely, and I wanted to say good-bye to *someone*.

Wait, there was someone I knew in New York City—Marlene Dietrich!

I had met Marlene in Hollywood at Billy Wilder's house. Billy had asked me to be her escort for the evening at his dinner party. We got along very well—too well! Afterward, she went back to New York and I stayed in Los Angeles.

I must have been irresistible when I spoke to her that day.

The interesting thing about Marlene was the more you needed help, the more attracted she was to you. I must have been irresistible when I spoke to her on the phone that day.

"Marlene, I'm on my way to Paris. It's my first trip to France."

"Who's taking you?"

"Nobody. I'm just waiting for my car."

"I'm coming over."

"No, no, no, the car will be here shortly."

"Wait for me." *Click!*

The car and Marlene arrived at the same time. She rode with me to the airport, helped me find my seat on the plane, and gave me a kiss as she handed me her St. Christopher medal. "This will bring you luck."

The medallion that Marlene gave me. I still have it.

Luck

They call it "luck."

It can't be taught.

It can't be borrowed,

Can't be bought.

It's more like destiny—or fate.

It may not find you, so

Do not wait.

Seize every moment.

Don't be deterred.

We make our own luck.

It's just a word.

Marlene Dietrich, *Shanghai Express.*

A scene from *Act of Love*.

I SPENT SOME TIME EXPLORING the wonders of Europe. By the time I arrived on set it was winter and the city was covered in snow. I was shooting a picture called *Act of Love*. One afternoon, the assistant director knocked on my door. He wanted me to meet the girl who was

It's just water.

working in public relations for the film. When I opened the door, I was introduced to a beautiful woman named Anne Buydens. It didn't take me long to decide to invite her to dinner with me. I suggested the Tour d'Argent, a very romantic restaurant in a penthouse overlooking Notre Dame Cathedral. After waiting for what seemed to be a long time for her answer, she smiled and said, "No, thank you, I'm awfully tired. I think I will just go home and make some eggs and go to bed."

When I opened the door, I was introduced to a beautiful woman....

My love turned to anger. I vowed to never speak to *her* again.

But . . . I did.

Since Anne was handling public relations it was difficult to avoid her—and I really didn't want to. Our relationship was civil but all business. I was pleasantly surprised when she accepted my next invitation to see the annual charity event of The Cirque d'Hiver in Paris. It was a true spectacle in which all of the French actors played the parts of the circus performers. As we approached the stadium the actors recognized me and begged me to join them: "Ah, Kirk Douglas, you must participate in our show."

I was taken aback. "What will I do?"

"We will find your talent."

"Anne, I will see you after the show!" I called out to her as they pulled me away.

Anne sat in a box watching the performance. Then it came time for my act. I looked out from behind the curtain to see the actors riding on elephants. As they left the arena, I came out alone in my tuxedo with a shovel and a broom and began cleaning up what the elephants had left behind. The audience roared!

Anne thought I was a big hit
As she watched me shoveling shit.

When I returned to find Anne, she was still laughing. At the end of the evening, she gave me a good night kiss, and, at that moment, I knew I had won her over.

Even though *Act of Love* ended, my feelings for Anne did not. My agent was urging me to come back to the United States for another picture but I was in no rush to leave.

Me and Anne.

One sunny day, Anne and I took a trip to Lido Beach, near Toulon. For some time I had been trying to persuade her to come back to Los Angeles with me for a visit. She was not very receptive, but I continued pressing my case.

Suddenly, Anne nudged me and pointed, "Look but don't touch." As I peered to where Anne was pointing, I saw the most beautiful girl in the world—long slim legs and everything that goes with it. As she approached, she looked at me and came running over crying, "Keerk!" *What? She recognizes me?!*

"C'est moi! Brigitte!"

Then *I* recognized *her*—Brigitte Bardot! She'd had a small part in *Act of Love*. In her war scene, the actors all wore heavy clothing. I remembered a cute little face, but I didn't imagine what all those layers were hiding! Brigitte Bardot soon became a sex symbol all over the world.

> Suddenly, Anne nudged me and pointed, "Look, but don't touch."

Look But Don't Touch

She knows me—
It's obvious I'm staring at
The beauty by the sea.
Voluptuous and sensuous, her mouth
The perfect pout.
The animal inside of her so hungry
To come out.
Anne knows me well enough to clearly read
My secret thoughts.
There's no use in denying it:
I know I have been caught.
I'm guilty of appreciating
Someone I don't know.
But what man could resist a look
At young Brigitte Bardot?

Brigitte, Brigitte,
Brigitte Bardot,

Why don't the boys
let you go?

They hang on to you
for as long as they can,

Until you escape with
another man.

Sixty years later I learned that Brigitte devoted her time to helping animals, which is a passion of mine as well. I wrote her a letter and sent a contribution to her charity. She was kind enough to answer me.

Yes, there were many beautiful girls in Paris, but the only one I was interested in was Anne. I continued with my campaign to convince her to come to Hollywood. Maybe she was tired of my nagging, but she finally agreed—sort of.

Yes, there were many beautiful girls in Paris but the only one I was interested in was Anne.

"All right Kirk, but I can only stay ten days."

"Why?"

"I have to be back in Paris."

I was happy with my partial victory. Now all I had to do was get her to stay longer.

How? I married her.

We rushed to Las Vegas with a few friends. The ceremony took place in a suite on the sixtieth floor of the Sahara Hotel. The preacher wore a cowboy hat and spoke with a drawl. He said to Anne, "Repeat after me: 'I, Anne, take thee, Kirk, as my lawful wedded husband.'" Anne repeated distinctly: "I, Anne, take thee, Kirk, as my *awful*

MAY 2012

My dear Kirk

I thank you a lot for your so nice
letter! I was very surprise you remember
me in my winter coat very horrible in
the film "un acte d'amour"_
It was one of my first movies and I was
very shy, but so happy to have a little part
with an actor international like you_
It was the first time in my life I meet an
american star like you! You were like God
for me!
On the beach in Cannes and Venizia you have
been like an old friend for me, I will always
remember!
You are an important part of my life and
I thank you now to love animals and
to want help my fight against the
barbarian way the human people
in the world are treating the animals
for money.
I send you some documents in french
and in english.
 I adore you and kiss you with all
my love_

                    B.B. Brigitte Bardot

wedded husband." The guests giggled. Anne was embarrassed and tried to explain, "I thought he said awe *full*—full of awe."

But we were married nonetheless.

I have made many mistakes in life. This was not one of them. Every day was happier than the one before. Every night was sheer bliss.

Without Her

Next to me lies a pillow
So soft, the color blue.
I crush the pillow to my chest
While I think of you.

I peer at the clock above my head
How long will I be alone in bed?
Wait! I hear her—

I throw the pillow on the floor.
Jump out of bed
And go for the door.

Soon you are in my arms
As I hold you tight.
Breath to breath, we are one
As we doze through the night.

Oh my darling, I love you
You make me feel so glad,
But the pillow lying on the floor
Is crushed and looks so sad.

With Anne.

With Peter.

With Eric.

WE SPENT A LOT OF TIME IN BED. We had two boys, Peter in 1955 and Eric in 1958. They joined my two older sons, Michael and Joel, from my first marriage to actress Diana Dill.

I met Diana when we were both in drama school. At that time, I was going with another classmate, Betty (Lauren Bacall). Diana kept advising Betty, "Kirk is the wrong guy for you."

After graduation, I went off to fight in World War II, but when I returned I looked Diana up in New York. I asked her out on a date and she suggested we go horseback riding. At that point I had never ridden a horse except for sitting on my father's horse, Bill, as he slowly trotted to the barn. But I said, "Sure."

We rented two horses and went riding in Central Park. I was having more than a little trouble when suddenly the horse threw me to the ground. Diana rode her horse around the park as I walked mine back to the stable. She didn't make fun of me, so I married her.

Diana and I had a good relationship, but it got better after we separated. Our divorce was not typical and certainly not typical in Hollywood. I told my lawyers, "Give

Diana anything she wants." Diana responded with: "No, Kirk has worked very hard." Later, she and Anne became very good friends; in fact, Anne calls Diana "our first wife."

Michael and Joel lived with their mother and her second husband, Bill Darrid, in New York. The boys would spend time with us during school vacations. All four boys got along well, but there was a distinct age difference.

Watching our children play.

Michael and Joel were ten years older and the younger boys would often trail behind them.

One summer evening, Anne and I watched the boys as they played in the yard. Suddenly, Eric, around five or six at the time, climbed up the tree to get into the treehouse I had built for the two older boys. Anne and I stood paralyzed as Eric fell out of the treehouse and onto the grass below.

"Oh my God!" Anne cried.

"I'm alright!" Eric said as he bounced back up to continue playing with his brothers.

Relieved, Anne turned to me and said, "Did you see that? He got up just like you do after a stunt. I think they will all become actors."

"I hope not," I replied.

"How can you say that? Don't you see how they play?"

"Well, all children are actors."

Actors? I'd like to see a lawyer or a doctor.

Actors Are Children

Actors are children,

Who refuse to grow up.

They live in a land of make-believe.

They play sailors, soldiers, and cowboys too.

They're happy when they deceive.

Hard work can get you fame and fortune,

And maybe make you a star.

But nothing will make you happy

Until you know who you are.

Peter taking care of Eric.

The gang's all wet.

AS MY FAMILY WAS GROWING, SO WAS MY CAREER.
I formed my own production company, Bryna (named after my mother), and one of the first projects I developed was based on a bestselling book—*Spartacus*.

Spartacus was made during the McCarthy Era. Senator Joe McCarthy accused Hollywood writers, directors, and actors of being Communists. Those who were accused were put on the "blacklist"; most lost their careers and some lost their lives. It was a terrible time in Hollywood. I helped to break the blacklist by giving screenwriting credit to my friend, the brilliant writer Dalton Trumbo, a blacklisted writer. I think the drama of getting Trumbo's name on the script was more dramatic than the movie itself.

The lines from my movies don't usually stay with me. There is, however, one beautiful bit of dialogue from *Spartacus* that I can still recite after fifty years. Trumbo wrote these lines for the love scene between Jean Simmons and me:

Spartacus falling in love with Varinia.

Spartacus:
I'm free. What do I know? I don't even know how to read.

Varinia:
You know things that can't be taught.

Spartacus:
I know nothing. Nothing! I want to know.
I want to . . . I want to know.

Varinia:
Know what?

Spartacus:
Everything. Why a star falls and a bird doesn't?
Where the sun goes at night?
Why the moon changes shape?
I want to know where the wind comes from. . . .
(Spartacus looks at Varinia longingly
and puts his arm around her)

Spartacus:
I want to know all about you. Every line,
every curve. I want to know every part of you.
Every beat of your heart.

MY CAREER TOOK ME AWAY FROM HOME A LOT. But when I could, I made sure my boys and Anne were with me. I always found my sons a job on my movies. Peter got his start on *The Vikings* when he was about three. He and Tony Curtis's daughter, Kelly, played children of the

MAKE-UP
ACTORS

Peter getting ready for
his close-up.

villagers. In one scene, a village person screamed, "The Vikings are coming! The Vikings are coming!" and grabbed the children and ran. Peter and Kelly were so terrified they started crying.

That was the end of Peter's acting career. When he was older he became a producer. One of his productions was my film *The Final Countdown*.

Peter and Kelly were so terrified they started crying. That was the end of Peter's acting career.

With *The Final Countdown* producer Peter Douglas.

Now we are in Israel filming
Cast a Giant Shadow.

My son Joel is a happy guy who makes everyone laugh. He was often my bodyguard on set. When I was filming *Cast a Giant Shadow* in Israel, I wanted to get my hair cut with a local barber. Joel, Anne, and I went to the barbershop. Within minutes, the shop was surrounded by fans. When the barber finished my haircut, we couldn't get out of the shop. Joel, leading the way, had us form a human chain to get to our car. Now he is a producer, but he is still my favorite bodyguard.

Eric, my youngest, was a loner who wanted to be an actor.

And Michael . . .

Michael is my oldest son. Growing up, he showed no interest in movies. Once though, I was able to persuade him to play the part of a young Israeli soldier who drove a jeep in *Cast a Giant Shadow* because Michael is an excellent driver. But throughout much of his early life he seemed to avoid me. Why? I tried to find out.

The family.

Michael

"Am I a good father?" I asked my son
He took a pause, too long for me
I waited and waited for him to answer
And finally he said, "Ultimately."

But the pause was all I heard
The silence was so loud
I was waiting for some kind word
Something that would make me proud.

How could I be so dumb?
That I never heard
The answer in the pause,
When he spoke not a word.

I became a "good father,"
It took me too long to see,
When I needed him
More than he needed me.

Eric, my youngest son, showed the most talent for acting. In 1991 we did a television movie together, *Tales from the Crypt: Yellow*. He was young and looking forward to a glorious future.

Unfortunately, he also battled addiction. Eric died from an accidental overdose of drugs when he was 46 years old. I blamed myself—and God—for taking him too soon.

Eric, my youngest son, showed the most talent for acting.

Counselors tried to help by constantly repeating this mantra, "You didn't *cause* it, you can't *control* it, you can't *cure* it." Nothing helped. There is no closure, and his passing remains a sad part of my life to this day.

Eric's grave lies in Westwood Memorial Park, a cemetery surrounded by high-rise apartments, where the residents can look down and see their final destination. My wife and I visit Eric often.

For Eric

I sit by your grave and weep,

Silently, not to disturb your sleep.

Rest in peace my beautiful son

It won't be long before we are one,

While I lie down by your side.

And talk, no secrets to hide.

Tell me, Eric, what did I do wrong?

What should I have done to make you strong?

Now I sit here and cry,

Waiting to be with you when I die.

I NEVER TRIED TO INFLUENCE MY BOYS in terms of their religion. Fortunately, I had two wives who felt the same way. Religion, or nonreligion, is a personal matter.

I believe in God—of course I do. I often walk around our beautiful garden to see the flowers, the trees, the green grass—all God's creations. In the middle of the garden sits my favorite bench. Years ago, in Palm Springs, Anne and I became friends with an artist named Kennedy. He built an iron bench of a man and a woman that sat on his patio. My wife loved that bench and convinced him to sell it to us. He did. Now I love it, too.

Sitting on the bench, I pick a rose from the garden—I see God! You plant a little seed in the ground, rain sprinkles down from the sky, waters the plants, and, eventually, you have a beautiful rose—perfectly shaped. What other proof do I need to know there's a God?

What other proof do I need to know there's a God?

My Friend

God walks beside me in the open air.

I can't see Him but

I'm sure He's there.

Together, we admire His green grass, His roses in bloom,

Tomorrow that red one will decorate my room.

Together we admire His palm trees,

Tinted silver by the setting sun.

A sudden breeze carries God away,

As light is fading at the end of day.

I sit there lonely, until it's hard to see,

So, I get up and—He is inside of me!

I'm happy to know that God is everywhere:

In the broiling sun, the pouring rain,

And in the cool night air.

Look for Him. He is your friend, too.

But if you can't find Him, He will find you.

LIFE IS NEVER EASY, but as I watched my hair turn silver, I was happy. I had a great career, many friends, and I was making more money than I ever dreamed of. Life was good. But then something devastating happened.

One day, while having a manicure, I was talking to Rose, the manicurist. Suddenly, I couldn't talk. I was babbling, making sounds but no sense. Rose called my wife, who immediately rushed to meet me at Cedar Sinai hospital, where I was told I'd had a stroke. I still couldn't talk. It struck me funny—"What does an actor do when he can't talk? Wait for silent pictures to come back?" But it wasn't funny.

I went home from the hospital depressed, deeply depressed. An actor who couldn't talk. What was my future? I thought of the many movies I had made; I was certain that there would be no more. I shuffled to my safe and opened it. I took out the gun I had used in the picture *Gunfight at the O.K. Corral* and saw that it was loaded. I stuck the barrel in my mouth—"Ouch!" I pulled it away. Then I began to laugh. A toothache stopped me from committing suicide.

Anne discussed the prognosis with my doctors. They suggested getting a speech therapist. They tried many. They finally decided on Dr. Betty McMicken.

When I first met Betty, she looked like a cowboy in full range-riding attire—boots, jeans, and a big leather belt. I scoffed at the idea that she could help me. She had just spent the afternoon riding in the mountains. *What the hell can she do for me?*

And then she started sending me poems. The fax machine spit them out every day, each poem containing lines full of polysyllabic phrases. Betty concentrated on the under-lined words and made me say this poem to start the speech process:

Betty McMicken.

Time to challenge my <u>elocution</u>
I will begin the <u>revolution</u>
To overthrow my mumble

Make this week of perfect diction
Eliminate the dereliction
That pervades with lack of practice
In the afternoon I will bellow
I'm an articulate and boisterous fellow
When I get my ass in gear
I shall work at voice production
As I build with strong construction
An octaves highs and lows
Lastly, I will wag and stick out my tongue
Stretch it out and be among
Those with deliverance charismatic
Not enigmatic

As in:
Mysterious, unknowable, inscrutable, unfathomable
I will be magnetic, compelling, alluring, fascinating,
Captivating, charming, appealing, attractive and reactive
When I speak the way I should
When the Issur in me is good
I can be quite entertaining!

—Dr. Betty McMicken

Betty was always in a happy mood while I scowled and grunted trying to read the poem and make sense of the long words. The more I complained, the cheerier she became, assuring me that I would talk again. The stream of poems began to intrigue me and I tried, with little success, to read them aloud. One day I startled myself—*I was talking*!—Not very clearly, but I could say some words that Betty understood.

One day I startled myself—*I was talking!*

In the car, being driven to the office, I practiced the speech exercises she gave me. At a red light my exercise of sticking out my tongue brought a response from the driver next to us who stuck out his tongue farther!

But miraculously, I began to talk—to the dismay of my household because Betty said, "Talk loudly, make it come from your gut!"

One afternoon, a four-year-old boy, Adam, skipped by the open door to my production office.

I stopped him, "Hey! How 'bout a high-five?" He came in, slapped my hand.

"What's your name?"

"Adam. What's yours?"

"Kirk. How old are you, Adam?"

He raised four fingers in front of my face and said, "Four!"

"How old do you think I am, Adam?"

He studied me seriously for a few moments and then he blurted out, "Twenty!"

I didn't dare frighten him by telling him how old I *really* was. But I was happy that someone could understand me.

My friend Adam.

BY NOW IT HAD BEEN WELL PUBLICIZED that I had difficulty speaking. All of my colleagues assumed I would never talk again. It was time to combat the rumors. At the age of 91, I started writing a one-man show, *Before I Forget.* When it was finished, I performed it at the Kirk Douglas Theatre in Culver City, California.

On stage after my stroke.

It was my first time performing onstage in over forty years, and the first time I had performed live since my stroke. To say I was nervous would be an understatement. I took every precaution—two teleprompters onstage in case I forgot my lines and comfortable chairs to sit down in, when I needed a rest. I even had two buckets backstage on either side, if I needed to urinate. The show was ninety minutes without an intermission so there was no time to go to the men's room.

> To say I was nervous would be an understatement.

Before opening night I scheduled a few workshop performances with my friends Larry Gelbart and John Lithgow. Larry wrote *Tootsie* and *A Funny Thing Happened on the Way to the Forum*, and John is an accomplished actor who had performed a one-man show as well. They enjoyed my performance, and, with their blessing, I was ready to open my show.

Opening night, the theater was packed. As I looked out from the stage, I spotted my sons with their wives; Tom Hanks, who came with his wife, Rita Wilson; Oliver Stone; and, of course, my beloved Anne.

Thankfully, I performed my show without a glitch. Relieved, I took my curtain call—a standing ovation— but then, my son Michael suddenly appeared onstage. I looked at Michael with his beaming smile and the crinkle of his eyes. He was handing me something. As I looked closer I saw that it was a vanilla ice cream cone—just like the ice cream cone that my father gave me the day of my very first performance. I hugged and kissed my oldest son.

I grabbed the cone as if it were an Oscar.

"Dad," Michael smiled, "the ice cream is melting."

I took the cone from him; ice cream had never tasted so sweet.

The show was a hit. I performed it four times and reached my goal—people now knew that I could speak well enough to perform. But the best part was getting that ice cream cone.

But the best part was getting that ice cream cone.

ALONG WITH MY ABILITY TO SPEAK, I also regained my ability to argue. Marriage is never easy for anyone. Anne and I have had many disagreements solved by a kiss.

Once, we had a particularly bitter quarrel. Anne wanted me to sell our vacation house in Palm Springs and buy a house in Montecito. But I wanted to stay in Palm Springs and play golf.

"Kirk, there are golf courses in Montecito!" Anne cried.

"I know that! But I don't want to make new friends. Anne, that's enough! We're going to stay here!"

Anne stormed out of the room, screaming, "Kirk I'm going to leave you!"

"You can't!"

Anne turned around, "Why not?"

"Because if you ever leave me, I'm going with you!"

Anne burst out laughing.

The next day we moved to Montecito.

Our fight inspired this poem:

Please Stay in Love with Me

Does fifty years together

Seem so long ago to you?

The older the violin, the sweeter the music

It is often said, and it's true.

To me, it seems like yesterday

We met in gay Paree.

Now Paris is sad, but I am glad

You chose to marry me.

In Montecito, we have
a beautiful garden filled
with roses and a big elm
tree. Each season our tree
was covered with gorgeous
leaves. Then, one spring, no
leaves appeared, and the elm
tree stood barren against the
sky. The gardener wanted to
cut it down, but I stopped him.

This tree still stands in our garden.

"But it's dead," he said.

"I think it's beautiful."

The gardener walked away, grumbling.

The great Indian philosopher and teacher Krish-
namurti wrote:

Have you ever noticed a tree standing naked against the sky,
how beautiful it is? All its branches are outlined, and in its
nakedness there is a poem, there is a song.

—Think on These Things

A minor poet like me wrote:

Trees

The trunks of trees are beautiful,

Pieces of sculpture to me.

The leaves are beautiful too,

But they are much easier to see.

The trunks are always there

Beneath the canopy they're found

Working to sustain beautiful leaves

Before they fall to the ground.

WHEN I TURNED 90, Anne threw me a surprise birthday party. She rented the entire L'Orangerie restaurant, our favorite haunt. A colorful mob came including Dominick Dunne, Jack Valenti, Merv Griffin, Don Rickles, Nancy Reagan, David Foster, Dennis Miller, Larry Gelbart, and Barbara Sinatra.

My friend George Schlatter, the producer, directed my sons in a song and dance routine, with a song written by his daughter:

Here is a man who
Is so very manly
Cleft upon his chin,
So deep you could dive in
My Poppa
My Poppa

I was overwhelmed by the festivities, but I didn't feel like I was 90 years old.

Many people stood up and gave tributes to Anne and I. I knew I would have to get up and say something—but

You are lucky you can't hear them.

what? I discarded the idea of one
of my poems. What could I say? Then it came to me—a
sonnet by William Shakespeare that I had learned years
ago. Would I still remember the words?

"Now we will hear from the guest of honor—Kirk
Douglas!"

I stood up, took a deep breath, and looked at Anne:

When, in disgrace with fortune and men's eyes,
I all alone beweep my outcast state,
And trouble deaf heaven with my bootless cries,
And look upon myself, and curse my fate,
Wishing me like to one more rich in hope,
Featur'd like him, like him with friends possess'd,
Desiring this man's art and that man's scope,
With what I most enjoy contented least;
Yet in these thoughts myself almost despising,
Haply I think on thee, and then my state,
Like to the lark at break of day arising
From sullen earth, sings hymns at heaven's gate;
For thy sweet love remember'd such wealth brings
That then I scorn to change my state with kings.

—*Shakespeare,* Sonnet 29

I looked around the room at all of our friends and family applauding wildly, except for Anne. She had tears in her eyes.

OF ALL THE PARTS I'VE PLAYED, I think I enjoy the role of "Pappy" the best. I love children; they see the world so differently. It's been a long time since my boys were young, but now I have a little girl—Victoria.

Leticia, her mother, is our housekeeper. She is family to us. After she had Victoria, I held that little bundle of humanity in my arms when she was baptized in church. I became her godfather.

Victoria is now thirteen years old and taller than I am. We have races in the swimming pool—and she beats me. I love to hear her running around the house.

Victoria at my door.

Victoria

Her little feet are running down the hall.

"Pappy!" She enters before I answer her call.

The morning paper is in her hand.

She places it on my bed.

She says not a word,

Gives me my glasses instead.

A quick kiss—and she turns on the light.

Before I can thank her, she's out of sight.

I have seven grandchildren. And I have loved watching all of them grow up.

Children (L to R): Jason, Kelsey, Dylan, Cameron, Kirk, Tyler, Carys, Ryan.

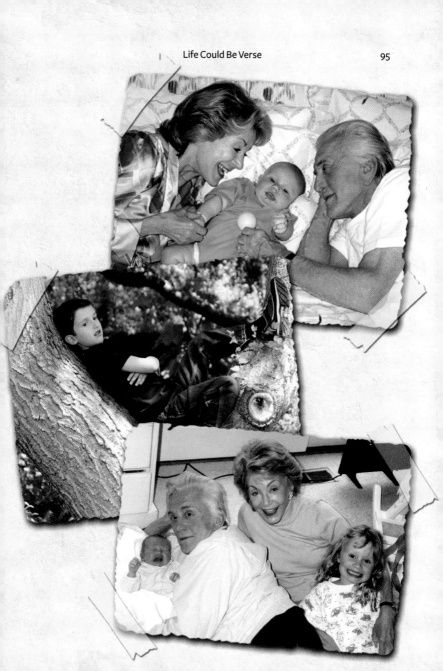

I tell this story often, but it's one of my favorites. When Cameron was a young boy he said to his father, Michael, "Dad, Pappy is Jewish, right?"

"Yes, one hundred percent."

"But what are you?"

"I guess I'm half Jewish."

"Oh. Then what am I?"

"Well, you're a quarter Jewish."

Cameron thought about that for a moment and then looked up at his father, "Dad, I wanna be half Jewish."

Three of my grandchildren (Kelsey, Tyler, and Dylan) have had bar and bat mitzvahs. I have gone to all of them. Kelsey's was first, and her rabbi was a woman. Kelsey is now studying at the University of Pennsylvania and dreams of becoming an actor. Tyler is also studying at the University of Pennsylvania with his sister, but he plans on becoming an engineer. Dylan loves music, and so his parents arranged a Rolling Stones/Beatles–themed bar mitzvah, which was great fun. He also wants to become an actor.

Ryan and Jason, my youngest grandsons, are busy playing video games and going to school. And Carys, Dylan's sister, is affectionate and bright. She is quite a poet herself.

Dear Pappy and Oma,

In school we have been learning a lot about poetry. I wanted to make a poem about you. I love you so much and I really hope you like it. I wrote from my heart and I didn't even need to write it down. That poem is about your love together and I thought I couldn't say it without poetry because your love is so strong I can't even put it into words.

Carys

Pappy and Oma

So beautiful together

Walking in the cool breezy night

Laughing together

Looking at the dark sky.

Seeing the twinkling stars winking back at them,

Sand between their toes soft as satin.

Oma with all her roses saw Pappy at the start.

They danced around saying,

I love you with all my heart.

—Carys

ANNE AND I LOOK FORWARD to our weekends in Montecito, a small coastal town north of Los Angeles. We both love the peace and quiet we find there. In the evenings, sitting around the fire, we talk. We call it our "Golden Hour."

As you get older, you are left facing each other as you really are—two human beings who have shared a life together.

As you get older, you are left facing each other as you really are—two human beings who have shared a life together.

Pappy and Oma in the Golden Hour.

By sharing a life with Anne, I discovered things about her I had never known. Gradually, she became a new, even more wonderful person to me. I fell in love with her all over again. Yes, at 80.

I also discovered that love is not a noun; it's a verb— full of action—kissing, cuddling, writing poetry, singing. It never stays still.

Romance Begins at 80

Romance begins at 80

And I ought to know.

I live with a girl

Who will tell you so.

I sit by her bath

As she soaks in the tub.

Then help her out

For a strong towel rub.

She likes that a lot

But before I tire.

It's time to pour the wine

And start lighting the fire.

As the fire crackles,

We talk of the past

We met 60 years ago

Did you think it would last?

The glasses are empty

The ashes are red.

Thanks for a lovely evening

But now it's time for bed.

I DON'T SEE MY SON MICHAEL often enough, so it was an unexpected pleasure even when he arrived at our door one day in 2014. He didn't say hello; he just started talking:

"Dad, I agree with what you've always said about 'Hallmark holidays.' I don't pay much attention to birthdays, Father's Day, Mother's Day, all of that stuff. They are all commercialized. But I came here to tell you that there's one event I really want to celebrate."

I was perplexed. "What's that, Michael?"

He smiled at me and at Anne, who had just entered the room.

"I want to celebrate two people who have lived together and loved each other for *sixty years*."

"Michael, you don't . . ." He cut me off.

"Dad, I don't want to hear it. This is important to us. Catherine and I will handle all the arrangements."

And they did. It was a magical evening.

The event was at the historic Greystone Manor in Beverly Hills where we celebrated our fiftieth a decade earlier by renewing our vows. Anne had surprised me by converting to Judaism as my anniversary gift. She explained, "It's time for Kirk to marry a nice Jewish girl."

The Greystone grounds had been transformed into an alfresco Cocoanut Grove–style nightclub. When we entered, Anne looked as glamorous as she had that first day she walked into my life in Paris. I was proud to be by her side.

We had never been so happy. I didn't know you got an award for living with a wonderful woman for sixty years— although she's the one who deserves it.

When we entered, Anne looked as glamorous as she had that first day she walked into my life in Paris.

A FEW WEEKS AFTER OUR ANNIVERSARY, I was sitting in our Montecito living room, staring at the fire and waiting for my wife. *Are women always late?*

Suddenly, Mary, our housekeeper, rushed in out of breath. "Mrs. Douglas fell down!" I ran to her. She was on the floor, crying in pain, all crumpled up. I shouted, "Somebody call 911!" The housekeeper had already done it. At that exact moment, six paramedics rushed past me and came to my wife's side. I watched helplessly as they gave Anne, still in tremendous pain, a morphine shot. They managed to get her on a stretcher and took her to the hospital. Thank God she was okay.

But her fall stunned me. It made me think about death. Anne refuses to talk about death. But I thought, *If she dies, I couldn't take it. I couldn't handle life without her. I must go first because she could handle that.* When you're married long enough, you learn that women are stronger than men.

> Let me go before my wife.
> Without her I have no life
> I'm sure that Anne will pray for me
> And we will live in eternity.

While Anne was recovering, I thought of what I could do to lift her spirits. Soon an idea began to take shape. Singing wasn't ever really my skill. The only songs I ever performed more than once were "Red Hot Henry Brown" and "Whale of a Tale," from the Disney movie *20,000 Leagues Under the Sea*. But I thought I could still perform a song for Anne.

Most songs you hear on the radio, television, or in the movies are written for young people—Elvis Presley singing, "Are You Lonesome Tonight?" Sinatra crooning, "What Is This Thing Called Love?" Paul McCartney's haunting lyrics and melody for "Yesterday." No one writes a song for people in their nineties—and no one that I know of, who's almost one hundred, ever wrote a song.

I decided that I would rework a song for Anne that I wrote for our fiftieth anniversary ten years earlier. The lyrics came first, then I found a melody that seemed to fit perfectly. But I didn't know what to do with it. So I called my friend David Foster, the brilliant songwriter and arranger, who lived in Malibu. I went to his studio and I asked him to record the song for me.

He looked surprised but said, "Sure, Kirk, why not?"

He sat down at the piano and I sang the song. He added some additional chords on the keyboard, and, within a few minutes, he wrote the music with the lyrics underneath. I immediately looked at the handwritten words. While they lined up perfectly, I hadn't even looked at the song in ten years. *Could I still do it?*

I found the lyrics and changed them to fit the moment. I practiced and practiced. And then practiced some more.

When Anne finally came home, I was scared. Did I dare sing to her? I hummed a little to prepare myself.

"What are you humming, darling?"

"Oh, I don't know."

I waited until nighttime. Sitting by her bed, I held her hand and cleared my throat. She looked up at me.

"Honey?"

"Yes, darling."

"I would like to sing a song for you."

She looked startled but said, "Go ahead." I cleared my throat and started:

You frightened me by falling

My own ground slipped away

God has brought you back to me,

He listened to me pray . . .

When you call me "angel"

I begin to sprout wings

Just whisper, "darling,"

And hear how my heart sings

I melt when you are near me

Like snow on a sunny day

Dissolve when you touch me

Like tear drops kissed away.

And if you ever leave me

I will follow you and cry

Please, darling, stay with me

Until the day I die.

As my voice trailed off, I looked over at her, and tears were pouring down her face. *She still loves me.*

IT IS A CLEAR SUNNY DAY IN MONTECITO. I walk around the garden that Anne and I built together, filled with the sculptures that we bought in our years of travel, the beautiful flowers, my favorite tree—I am happy.

I sit on my bench.

> "Take me, God, I'm ready to go
> I've lived almost 100 years
> I want a new adventure,
> Take me, I have no fears.
> I'm grateful for all you've given me
> on this beautiful earth below.
> Lots of fame and too much money—
> Now I'm ready to go."

"Kirk!"

That's my wife calling me.

I watch Anne slowly head back to the kitchen with her walker. She turns, "Lunch is ready, dear."

"God, let's wait another year."

I hurry to her and give her a kiss.

Life could be verse.

This is how it all started 60 years ago, the day after our wedding.

Photo Credits

Page 10. Courtesy of St. Lawrence University.

Page 16. She Done Him Wrong. Publicity image © by Paramount Productions, Inc. Courtesy of Universal Studios Licensing LLC.

Pages 22 and 23. The Strange Love of Martha Ivers © by Paramount Pictures Corporation. All Rights Reserved.

Pages 24, 25, 26 and 27. Champion © by Paramount Pictures Corporation. All Rights Reserved.

Pages 28, 29 and 30. Ace in the Hole © by Paramount Pictures Corporation. All Rights Reserved.

Pages 32 and 33. Devil's Disciple © 1959 Metro-Goldwyn-Mayer Studios Inc. All Rights Reserved Courtesy of MGM Media Licensing.

Pages 34 and 35. Detective Story © by Paramount Pictures Corporation. All Rights Reserved.

Page 39. Shanghai Express. © 1932 Paramount Publix Corporation, Courtesy of Universal Studios Licensing LLC.

Pages 40 and 41. Act of Love © 1953 Benagoss Productions, Inc. All Rights Reserved. Courtesy of MGM Media Licensing.

Page 47. Brigitte Bardot. © SIPA/Sipa USA.

Page 52. Courtesy of Roddy McDowell.

Page 55 and 59. Courtesy of Arthur Zinn.

Page 61. Spartacus. © 1991 Universal Studios Inc. All Rights Reserved.

Pages 63 and 64. The Vikings © 1958 The Bryna Company. All Rights Reserved. Courtesy of MGM Media Licensing.

Page 65. Final Countdown © 1980 Polyc International B.V. All Rights Reserved. Courtesy of MGM Media Licensing.

Page 66. Cast A Giant Shadow © 1966 Metro-Goldwyn-Mayer Studios Inc., Llenroc Productions and Batjac Productions, Inc. All Rights Reserved. Courtesy of MGM Media Licensing.

Page 76. Courtesy of Dr. Betty McMicken.

Page 79. Courtesy of Tali Silon.

Page 84. Courtesy of William Reed Woodfield.

Page 93, 94. Family. Courtesy of Christopher Briscoe.

Page 95. Tree. Page 96. Ryan. Courtesy of Christopher Briscoe.

Page 99. Bar Mitzah. Courtesy of Infinity-Kornfeld Studios.

Page 99. Grandsons. Courtesy of Christopher Briscoe.

Pages 106, 107 and 108. Family. Courtesy of Christopher Briscoe.

Page 114. Oma and Pappy (bottom right). Courtesy of Christopher Briscoe.

All other photos of the Douglas family are taken from the Douglas family private photo collection.

Lyrics

Page 17 and 18. Red Hot Henry Brown by Fred Rose. © 1925 (Renewed). EMI FEIST CATALOG INC. All rights controlled by EMI FEIST CATALOG INC. (Publishing) and ALFRED MUSIC (Print). All Rights Reserved.

Page 19. Lonely Town (from On the Town) by Leonard Bernstein. Lyrics by Betty Comden and Adolph Green. © 1945 Warner/Chappell. Leonard Bernstein Music Publishing Company LLC, Publisher. Boosey & Hawkes, Inc. Sole Agent. All Rights Reserved. International Copyright Secured. Reprinted by permission of Boosey & Hawkes, Inc.

Illustrations

Page 50. Artist: Lehr and Black.

Pages 3, 6, 12 and 116. Artist: Larissa Hise Henoch.